The James Downs Book of Poems

LOW TEMPLES

JAMES DOWNS

Copyright © 2022 by Joyce Downs
ISBN: 978-1-63649-692-4

All rights reserved. No part of this book may be used or reproduced in any manner whatsoever without written permission, except in the case of quotes for personal use and brief quotations embedded in critical articles or reviews.

Poetic Matrix Press
www.poeticmatrix.com

Low Temples

Ackowledgments

There's a Piece Missing From My Heart — Joyce Downs

When James and I were dating, he would always have a pen. He would scribble poems on napkins at dinner. He told me that he once wrote a poem on a balloon. He was very adamant that he would not write poetry on a computer. I gave him a journal. He later mentioned that that journal opened his heart to me, that I was more then just a nice lady in the TV room, where we first met.

'Yes, there is a piece missing from my heart. But, James mended numerous broken pieces along the way.

I will always love James. He has a piece of my heart, and I have a piece of his.

James went on to write hundreds of poems on his computer.

— John Peterson

This book is a gift to all of us from James and a gift from Joyce and myself to James. So many of us found James to be such a good and constant friend, and such a man. We miss him deeply and always. Poetry is one artistic form that is the truest part of a person to live on because it comes from the heart. This came from James' heart.

From the title poem, **Low Temples**.

> low temples   reached by quiet decision
> everywhere   around us   and yet
> we do not enter low temples
>
> low temples flow from us

Many of James' pieces had no title but were set-up in groups. I have tried to follow that here. So, if pieces have no titles that is his option, they are grouped according to the original manuscript.

This volumn was put together in honor of James Downs by Joyce Downs and John Peterson.

Dedication

To Joyce

As Always

Contents

LOW TEMPLES

Amber Blue	1
Breathe	2
Contents	3
Hope Is A Bird	4
Let Fly	5
Low Temples	

Memento Poems

Memento	9
flute melody	10
harpstrings	11
the sound it makes	12
crystal under hill	13

Mountain House Poems

Mountain House	17
shirt tucked in tightly	18
Perchance	19
making her feet rub	20
Cold Play	21
Thick	22
Stained Glass Horizon	23
Fuller	24
in the bones of the world	25
bowls of rice placed	26
Music Floats	27
Next	28
Oxygen	29
Procession	30

Questing Poems

I-Music	35
Ii–Calm Miind	36
Rain	37

Reach Poems

reach toward the earth	41
If i could find it	42
through the gaps in	43
React	44
Slept In The Fields Poems	45
my brain races	46
worked it out	47
the birds have no place to go	48
silver tint upon	49
across mountain meadow	50
within the breakers at ocean shore	51
sequoia trees have long memories	52
seated around a campfire we	53
rings circle fingers	54
coyote circles endlessly	55
we sit in sandpaper reeds	56
early morning silence	57
caked on mountain cliffs	58
mountain ridge balanced	59
If A Poem Were A Vote, If A Vote Could Be A Poem	60
Stuck	62
Transfer	63
Swimming In The Same Ocean	64

Amber Blue

out into the blue
you passed to me
        a book-journal to
fill in the blanks
        of my continuing life

you accepted
        my amber heart
and hung it to your chest
near enough
        to feel it beating

out into the blue
and back you passed on
        something of you
and we share
        in its continuing

Breathe

the wind picks up and dies down
along a line of clear force

as the wind moves   so the grasses
and every still attached pine leaves
move

when we breathe   the air displaces
for a moment   then replaces

I hadn't taken enough time
to walk among   these giants
lately

within the circling forces of nature
the wind drives home its nature

working upon   a deep breath pattern
one tries to get onto an even keel
line

as the wind picks out its path
so too do we breathe   we breathe

Contents

on early morning slate of sun
is written this day's light
and what is to be done

with it   how it traverses
how it supplants the shade
of previous night's darkened blade

across previous day's way   is
to be determined   we don't
really know the exact line

this day's content will take
for there is always one way
and certainly another in its wake

the slate is rubbed clean
and black by night's memory
erasure but in the morning there is

day and light and common pleasure

Hope is a Bird

hope is a bird that floats in on its
wide flimsy stained glass wings

and settles on your softened shoulders
waiting   hope doesn't know that any

thing is impossible   it sits there
with a clear body of anticipation

and waits   it waits for you to fling
aside all caution   it waits for you to

create a palette of emotion   that
will drag you to your leaden feet

it waits for brittle wings inside you to   unfold
and beat   shake and stretch   bring forth dreams

hope sits on tinted shoulders   quiet
internal   focused   bird-contained

and waits for you to sing

Let Fly

muddy water   i
   cannot see clearly   like
that old blues song

i just can't get through   how
   many times must i
be stuck inside something

that i wouldn't do if i
   were centered and true   so
focus on the subject

lens racheted   clear click
   and let fly   this is why
a calm repose   unforced mind

gets out of the way   lets
   the universe say exactly
what it wishes to say

and that is enough   well no
   that is everything   stay
within yourself and yet

in the same breath
   play out into the stars
reel out all the line

that you have   clear the water
   who knows the magnificent
wondrous things   you find

Memento Poems

Memento

wind   brushes   garden
sands in precise ess curves

within this natural   ritual
there is a precise moment

memento   ceremony

each of us that walk
through the garden

have need of eyes to see
inside where our sands

match that of the earth
wind   brushes back and forth

garden sands turn
        in precise ess curves

flute melody   koto plucking
backs across space   in the song
a place we have left   in our hurry

to move along life's driving throng

too soon   too soon we find the end
is just   an altering beginning
plaintive flute caressing koto spaces

to inhabit and keep   our souls alive

harpstrings   vibrate   in the wind
   tuningforks   of the world

our world is right and wrong at once

our instrument is finetuned
   and sensitive   and fragile

as the world keeps us there
   so too the spirit   hovers here

chimings bells that call us   call us

harpstrings vibrate   the wind like
   tuningforks   for our world

the sound it makes   the sound it makes
only scratches an itch upon the surface

deep in the sound it makes   is a fire
that never burns out   never burns as

bright as when it is playing
each one joins the whole   each one

wholly joins   never looks back   only
goal is to intermingle in   one   single   moment

then another   the sound it makes scratches
the surface and digs down to that fire

deep in the sound it makes   music

crystal under hill
    picking digging searching still
in hand already

Mountain House Poems

Mountain House

Thickets sticking to the skin
I remember going in   and
coming outside again

along the earth grubbed and
dirted I crawled and played
entering into this day's diary

few small things I have to say
bees and birds overhead
flee   an aviary of the perplexed

doubt   scepticism   form of
all forms   word structure permed
into some semblance of permanence

tangles touching the tongue
brushed one single verb "done"
if I have any chance

of coming undone   I would untie
all my shirtstrings   slip to the
earth and   dance   dance   dance

shirt tucked in tightly
   wind jumbles up our yard   lifts
me slightly off-ground

Perchance

digging into tilled earth
i pick out a bulb of indetermined
girth hold it in my hand   rub it
for all its worth   shine it like a penny
many plants hug this earth   in stances

of life-and-death perchances

pulling bulb by bulb up   i don't
have my syntax right   these plants
are pining for their soil   their water and
their light   gingerly   tenuously   i
put them back   bulb by bulb and

cover them with blankets of fresh earth

making her feet rub
   against my leg   my sweet lover
smiles mischieviously

Cold Play

out in the woods   stellar's jay
calls for anyone to answer
he becomes iritated   and his caw

soon sounds out the piercing scrape
of a saw   then he jabbers to himself
just to hear himself think

stellar's jay has been lonely all day

he floats from tree to pine tree   a ghost
not certain where he should be
stellar's jay jaws about his predicament

and the flaws in the universe

he calls out one more time
hoping he was just mistaken
it has taken way too long

stellar's jay is alone: all his friends are gone

Thick

rich sweet earth
pulls up to heights
worth all the Chinese tea

thick clumps of wet moss
cling to sides slick from pouring
water raining to meadows below

tall pine trees shoot out
to mid-air and dare gravity
paint-by-numbers fills

the sky with blue hue and cry
all the earth is why we are here
and we don't have else to go

rich sweet earth
pulled up to heights
proud and thick and worthy

Stained Glass Horizon

valley antiquity
      autumn drops
everything in its focused
      goal: winter-
proofing   yet for
      one single moment
all brilliance breaks out
      stained glass
horizon echoed in each
      leaf   each
tree   washing away
      slowly   tenderly
microcosms   for a season

Fuller

each of the slates of the mountain
overlap   touch   and plate
in mountain techtonics   shifts
and cracks of the cold and of the water

mountain slips across its space

if a mountain sits silent   it is
only from true contemplation
granite constitution   slick rock
natural combination of smile and grace

mountain crouches in its path

as time goes   mountain grows inches
the ditches and tracks stretch further
the sky gets closer   the earth becomes fuller
and horizon goes chasing past

mountain stops and steps in place
mountain lets its words   flow from its face

in the bones of the world
are trapped the sounds of life

it is a set of tones   modulated
and moaned out with distinct
precise   skeletal   brilliance

we feel the trembling   as we
shower   as we walk   as we
take each bite of daily food

in the bones of the world
lifesounds chime up and down

we shiver if we are listening
most human of tuning forks
waiting for our orchestra to play

then universe conducts the upbeat

bowls of rice placed
in a straight line
food and ritual as one
we honor the rice fields
we honor the ceramic earth
we honor our selves
as we place bowls of rice
in a straight line

Music Floats
     — for coco montoya blues band

music floats
across the surface of a cold cold glass
in a sluice   that is

melting   I'm melting
back into water   like
an ice cube

waves roll   over and over
my ears   my hearing
arranges notes into

revolving rhythms
cycling across the tabletop
music floats

across the surface of a cold cold glass
and echoes as vibrations hop
across my body

Next

what is it that we see
when we look far over horizon?

how are we to know the heart
of a stellar's jay or a ground squirrel?

where does the bear go when
we are sleeping at night?

if the apple falls from the tree
will there be someone to pick it up?

as we forget the things of the past will
there be things of the present to remember?

do we truly know everything
that we think we know?

why does a sleek bird fly through our life
at the precise moment we wish to fly?

getting in the boat, will we
find it is sealed and seaworthy?

is the going out sufficient
to the going in?

what is it that we see
when we look far out over horizon?

Oxygen

sun pulls up
      has no winter coat
dims its light in a pulling in

one's breath fog
      rings his head
hogs cold air of its oxygen

on the ess curve
      edge of a creek
december geese sit with silence

one cannot go out
      without surely
coming in   with air cold and clearing

Procession

the trees are changing
at different rates
the plate of colors
is rich   balanced
like life on the
upper end of
the juggler's stick

keeping things in the air
there are ways to describe
the move down the season

each plant pulls in
puts up   stains its leaves
with washes of color
brilliance   depth
before   jettison
becomes   drawn   bare

on and on   the juggling
spins the earth   keeps
trees   animals   dreams
turning on regular
course   tied to the world
and to living direction

without circling force   we all
would fly off in different directions
like scattered angry catthe trees are changing
but in regular procession
of the season   one would never
ask the trees to stop the color burst

before the losing   of leaves
for the splash leads to sleep
before wake up in spring

each plant spins its season
colors shooting off the plate
but the tree stays up there
we all stay up there   balanced
until green shoots up the stem
and starts us all over again

trees   splash   wash
pull in   jettison and
stay up on those sticks

Questing Poems

I--Music
— for the people of The People's Temple

we have a way to go
we can go along a throughline
finding bits and pieces of ourselves
on the way   we never knew the burden
until we carried it   we have a way to go

we came together for release
we came together for music   soaring
we came together for a peace we never
found anywhere along the throughline

we feel more and more there is no more place
for us to be   to go   than here   but what is here
but us   we came together in peace but we
dispersed in violence face down   in the jungle
that the world can be   we have a way to go

before a different version can be written   and yet
along the way we have a chance   picking up the bits
picking up the pieces   and picking up the people
along the throughline of the world   and yet
we have a way to go

II--Calm Mind
>   —for tenzin gyatso, 14th Dalai Lama
>   (the destruction of your neighbor is the
>   destruction of your self)

you need special care   carelessness
banished to the rubbled borders
of Tibetan heart/mind   he rubs his
balding head in thought   and centers
peace in his protected skull   there
there is spiritual riches amidst the rubble
and searches for meaningful autonomy
within   a bedrock of unity in this world

stability from looking within   within
each and every living soul   you need
special care everywhere   a new reality
anchored in each defined   whole

in a bowl of honored rice   along a line
of railway link   he welcomes these things
in his heart   he rubs his head   dreams of
going home to his people   to be with them
one   needs   special   care

Rain

rain   rain   rain
dropping
earth sucks it down in
sustenance
        soon to fly
to disperse in air again
rain   a thirsty drink
     of quenching water
earth's reason   purpose
      to raise things up
earth's core   growing things
rain   rain   drops
      fills my eyes full
and overflowing

Reach Poems

1

reach toward the earth
tree grows as root grows
sustenance is a long hard drink of water

if we think too much
we will never see the color
of our feelings reach full tint

when trees and humans encounter
isn't it better one offers shade
and the other accepts it?

maybe the tree is grounded
in the earth   but truly
a tree reaches for the stars

and what a better way
than to hold on yet let
go all at the same time

2

If i could find it
*   i could figure what*
it is   it is
*   and I wasn't even trying*

3

through the gaps in
window blinds slats   i see
clear air and brisk sun bathed
light   the fact that I see is in itself
wondrous   one kind of calm

through the gaps in my
walking   breathing   moments
i see clearly   calmly reach my self

React

tall reeds sway back and forth in breeze
if this happens   breathe just breathe

we will never know   what comes next
no matter   just breathe   if wind

bends grasses flat   and trees react
vacillating at the source   relax
be your own force   and breathe

breathe   oh just   breathe

      – for Joyce

Slept In the Fields Poems

slept in the fields
if you must sing do it quietly
for i am dreaming another song to the fore
there is a rich rhythm encircling me and i don't
want to drop the beat   sing quietly for i am afraid
that i will forget my song when i awake
but something tells me
that the rest of my life is this song   and we can both
sing it together   quietly   harmoniously
out in the fields

my brain races
too much stimulation: caffeine computer
but thinking is what i do   yet
the wind sweeps through like a handbroom
and clears my mind of thought
            and then i become a fan to whisk
unnecessary dust from my life   and
my brain stills   quiets   and calms

worked it out
    one moment at a time
the star keeps on going forward
    and hovers over my head
no animals gather
    no kings come bearing gifts
the manger is filled with only hay
    but i've worked it out
i'm here and i'm supposed to be
    and being is what i'm supposed
to do one moment at a time

the birds have no place to go
it is not the season for leaving yet
and not the season of coming back
so the birds just hang about and
          realize that they can play

if you've ever seen them divebomb
each other through the thin spray
of a waterfall only to jet straight up
and over again and over again you
          know that they can play

we are in between seasons   between
the comings and the goings
the backwards and the forwards
the thens and the nows   so when will we
          understand what play is

and play as if our life depended upon it?

silver tint upon
    window in hall   breath blown out
short purposeful puffs

across mountain meadow
lone mule deer grazes with a vengeance
muzzle chewing furiously
he grabs subsistence as if they were
the last grasses   they might be for we
have been careless and crumbling   altogether
blind to brother earth   there is a song sung
in each act committed   there are verses
and choruses we all commit to memory
the mule deer knows the song   the meadow
hears the song each day   echoing off the
mountain walls   across mountain meadow
mule deer still grazes   we are still careless
but if we listen we can hear the song
echoing around   and sing along

within the breakers at ocean shore
tiny living beings tumble
their lives turned upside down
over and over   they struggle
with all their lifeforce to survive
just one more wave and i will breathe
i will catch a breath and hold on

we are at that shore   relaxation   stillness
and soon we float to the top and above us see
a blue blue sky

sequoia trees have long memories
they store up in their rings all
that has happened before them for centuries
chinese vikings columbus
    spanish conquistadors monks
        westward moving pioneers
and in their pulpy flesh is registered all
that has passed before them and still the only
sound they make is swishing in their leaves
and branches creaking   and cones crackling
open to spread new seeds

seated around a campfire we
have stories to share about our lives
some choose to embellish embroider
others prefer the bold unvarnished tale

the sparks of flame venture up to the heavens
and our ancestors hear and approve or disapprove

rings circle fingers
    silver smithy stone fractures
circled and set free

coyote circles endlessly
looking for the just right
soft place to sleep
the three-quarters moon
shines over his shoulder
highlighting his little feet
coyote has not had rest
since he last could eat
and he is not sure when
that will be   but he will
be always bold   bright
in a winter's moon

we sit in sandpaper reeds
at water's edge preparing
for we know not what
the rough reeds smooth
our fingertips and cull out
other wasted plants   the breeze
hits our faces like low setting
on a box fan   and the river rolls
roils and pans across this quiet land
we sit here amongst a forest of reeds
present   attentive   focused
waiting

early morning silence
    staying up all night
writing poetry
    i get back further than
my genetic memory
    all the way back to
my soul's starting place
    touched by it   in sleepy
reverence   I am touched
    by something bigger than
my face

caked on mountain cliffs
the moss clings dearly
the moss sucks down
waters flowing from
an uphill source a creek
above from snowmelt
drain-down the mountainside
the moss cannot predict when
the creek will dry up
the moss only does its thing
clings and drains and greens

mountain ridge balanced
　　　through light drink-glass　　country view
half full or empty?

If a Poem Were a Vote,
If a Vote Could Be a Poem

then readings would be a plebiscite
and a poem would be an absentee ballot
turned in on time and filled out correctly

a poem turned about on word processor page
would be one of many democratic statements
of freedom and the search for truth

if a poem were a vote then each one shared
with a friend would be a strong campaign appeal
standing in the yard   sign ready to stick into the ground

a poem is always an appeal   trying to connect
finding the common   real   experience
just the statement a clear vote makes

if a vote could be a poem   then the collective wish
would become metaphors on a large page
like tabulations at election day's end

a vote among many   would be a poem about the sky
or an earth applause   or a quiet conversation between
two concerned citizens   contemplative meditations

if a vote were a poem we would connect directly
to all the tucked way anxieties or dreams
a vote would poem out into the world

a vote is always an appeal   connected to the
populace   real statements of the common weal
a clear long poem rolling out our hopes

if a poem were a vote   if a vote could be a poem
the nation would become   poets and voters
as one   philosophy flowing in common conversation

Stuck
— remembered history

within its structure
of windows and openings
I can see out   on the

other side there is a
click and a glottal stop
someone is warming up

their dormant vocal
chords to speak   I hadn't
taken any of this into

consideration   I had chosen
to stay where I was   frozen
in a time that wasn't really

of considered value   one just
gets into these places
and it is tough to get back out

within window and opening
structures   stuck   well then

listen to those about to speak
look for a door   and then go out

Transfer
                – for Sandy

across a space
   of air my friend
and I share her works

her blood   her words
   flowing from the tip
of her tongue of her mind

and from her soul   matching
    line for line   we
line up   click into place

friend by friend
     across the universal
space   we   share

Swimming In the Same Ocean

touched by this   vibrant
vibrating   current   we become
electric eels   darting   then flowing

searching in the source   searching
through the same water   touched
by the same waves   we bob between

them   blue sky   then water   then
blue sky   then water   one and another
if we'd keep our eyes wide open   everywhere

we are   swimming in the same ocean
we reap benefits of
             the universal mind

between waves   between waves   between waves
on this   blue   blue   planet

Author Biography

James Downs passed away on October 10, 2020 after an illness. My love to Joyce and his family and I miss him terribly. A friend likes James is a great gift and I cherish the time we had together. Our press project would not have existed without James.

I met James shortly after starting work in Yosemite National Park. Meeting James was a fortuitous event. We began meeting at Degan's Deli for morning lattes and began conversations that continued for months and then years. We talked about myriad topics including philosophy, politics, music, literature, and poetry. His depth and ease of conversation was enlivening and eventually lead to beginning Poetic Matrix Press. James had been creating small handwritten poetry books (3 X 4 inches) of his poetry. We went on to do chapbooks and over 80 full length books, including his book Merge with the River.

During this time James met Joyce and their love blossomed. Laurene and I had the great privilege of hosting their wedding on our property in Madera, California. They were wed under a giant Willow Tree by the creek with 70 friends and family. What a joy this day was. They eventually bought a place in Sonora and with Joyce's daughters lived a good life.

Needless to say, Joyce misses James profoundly. They met each other later in life and were graced with many beautiful years together. James told me many, many times how lucky he was to have found Joyce and how great his love for her was. I'm sure that love continues in this crazy universe we inhabit. Love truly does go on.

John Peterson, friend

www.ingramcontent.com/pod-product-compliance
Lightning Source LLC
Chambersburg PA
CBHW020951090426
42736CB00010B/1361